THIS BOOK IS DEDICATED TO ALBERT R. PUDVAN

FOREWORD

Ever wonder when you see a city on a map, "Why here?" Sometimes the answer is obvious. A conspiracy of geography and economics. Royal edict. Natural resources. All these are good reasons to start a city, but what keeps it growing and alive?

Part of the answer may lie in what Chicago has become. Proud, young, aggressive, reaching, daring, experimenting, redefining and remaking itself again and again. Attractive qualities that draw and keep people here.

Cities are like fountains. Fountains exist only so long as water flows through them. They change their temperament with the subtleties of the water. Cut off the water and they become inert statues of stone. Cities exist as long as people live in them. If there is nothing to pull people here and give them hope - the city, too, becomes nothing more than stone. Give people free reign of energy and expression, and the city surges upward without bound.

Even the buildings testify to that. The Sears Tower, which is visible from every corner of the city and beyond, is itself a city in miniature. It defies gravity hurling millions of tons of steel 1454 feet into the restless Midwest skies. Seventy-eight football fields of floor space are woven together with 43,000 miles of telephone cable, providing workspace for 11,000 people. Biggest, most, largest, best... Chicagoans wouldn't have their showpiece any other way.

Ask them. Ask each and every person in Chicago. You may get 4 million answers but they will have a number of things in common. Their direction is pointed to by the Sears Tower -Their limits are its infinite horizon.

That's why they are here. Over the years a limitless, flowing spirit has grown here. It's not because of a caprice of weather or an accident of history. When that spirit arrived, Chicago had to grow here.

Jay Flynn

A LONG
LONG TIME AGO

PRODUCED, PHOTOGRAPHED AND PUBLISHED BY: DAVID J. MAENZA

WRITTEN BY: JAY FLYNN

DESIGNED BY: JAMES GROLL

ART DIRECTION BY: PAUL COLLINS

EDITED BY: BOB HALE AND JEANETTE RAWLEY

POST PRODUCTION: GAMMA PHOTO COMPANY

PRODUCTION ASSISTANCE BY: CHRISTINE GROLL

PHOTO EDITOR AND MANAGER: JOANNE FILIPPI

ASSISTANT PHOTO EDITOR AND DESIGNER: SYDNEY GROLL

CONTRIBUTING PHOTOGRAPHERS: FRANCOIS PARIS, VIC BIDER, TONY CIMINO

TRAVEL AND TECHNICAL ADVISER: ROSE SCANDURA

ASSOCIATE EDITOR: DARLENE FICKE

ENTERTAINMENT AND RESTAURANT ADVISER: MARINA CHRISTIANSEN

FOOD PHOTOGRAPHY BY: MICHAEL COMACHO

BLACK AND WHITE PHOTOGRAPHY COURTESY OF THE SPECIAL COLLECTION DEPARTMENT, CHICAGO PUBLIC LIBRARY,
AND THE DAVID R. PHILLIPS ARCHIVES

djmpub@cbipc.com

Chicago was incorporated as a town on August 12, 1833 with a population of 350. When this photograph was taken, the city was just 55 years old.

Cities are living things. Chicago's birth hides in legend and dim history. Like many cities it took its first halting steps, faltered and picked itself up again. Chicago had an unruly adolescence and then it died. Few living things rise again, especially when struck down so young. Chicago did. Not content to remain forgotten in the past, Chicago worked to fulfill a seemingly impossible future vision.

Wrigley Building and Michigan Avenue Bridge, 1900

City Neighborhood, 1865

"Back in the 1920's, my late father used to compete against Johnny Weissmuller in Chicago River marathon swims."

Norman Ross
Radio Personality

State Street, 1893

The first people to settle along the green shores of the glacier-carved lake were the Illinois Native Americans. Their name for the place near the mouth of a slow river was Chicaugou. The name encompasses nothing of the city's future greatness. It means "wild onions" which grew along the marshy shoreline.

Mecca for Immigrants, 1910

Europeans first heard of Chicago from explorers and missionaries like Joliet and Marquette. Fort Dearborn was established at what is now the corner of Michigan Avenue and Wacker Drive. The first permanent European settler was Jean Baptiste Point Du Sable, a man of Franco-African descent. Du Sable came to Chicago because it stood at the head of the main trails to the unsettled west. Prophetically, he came here to trade.

Culture comes to the "Hog Butcher to the World" -- The Art Institute ca. 1920

The Reborn City grows: Turn- of-the-century parade on South Michigan Avenue

Through the early and middle 1800's the city boomed. Grain flowed out on newly built railroads. Irish, Poles, Germans, fleeing starvation and tyranny in Europe, and newly-freed African-American slaves flooded the town and Chicago sprawled into a city. Then one searing October night in 1871, the city died.

Michigan Avenue south from Chicago Avenue

Planners like Burnham and Sullivan saw an opportunity to replace disease-plagued sprawl with a model city. URBS IN HORTO, A CITY IN A GARDEN became the motto of the reborn Chicago. Its centerpiece was to be the lake shore, not acres of stone.

Chicago's Front Yard: Grant Park and "Boul Mich" District, South Michigan Avenue, 1940s

The lake shore was given over to almost 25 miles of park and recreation land, Chicago's Front Yard. Inside the city itself, 560 parks testified to the motto.

State Street becomes "that Great Street", 1900

Daring architecture took root and stretched to the sky. Chicago is the birthplace of the first skyscraper and first elevated train line. Today, the works of Sullivan, Burnham and Wright stand beside those of modern architects. Mies Van Der Rohe made Chicago a proving ground of gleaming dreams in steel and glass.

Sears Tower under construction, 1979

Sears Tower stands as a milestone to the modern era of Chicago. Still the tallest building in the world in two official categories, Sears Tower stretches from the primeval limestone to the clouds. In its superlatives it represents leaps over countless structural obstacles that daunted those with smaller visions.

Topping this architectural giant is Sears Tower Skydeck -- "Chicago's Highest Attraction". At 1,353 feet above the ground, this world-class observatory offers stunning views covering all of Chicago and four states. High speed elevators whisk guests 103 stories skyward in just 70 seconds to where floor to ceiling windows offer unobstructed views in all directions. Since its opening on June 22, 1974, Sears Tower Skydeck has welcomed more than 30 million guests from around the world.

Sears Tower looms 1,450 feet above street level. On a clear day, parts of Illinois, Michigan, Indiana and Wisconsin can be seen from the Skydeck.

Chicago is a living museum of architecture. Walking tours criss-cross the city, showing visitors experiments and achievements of both the past and present as cranes nurse new construction skyward.

Chicagoans often play a game of guessing what a new building will look like. A castle, a geometric spire or even a wedding cake are some of the suggestions as a new iron gridwork takes shape. As the City grows, it is hard to imagine that it was nothing but ashes about 130 years ago.

"Having traveled all over the world, I know of no other city that takes as much pride in itself as Chicago. The vitality and talent of the people... and the energy, the beauty of this city, just excite me. And the climate... well, it makes you strong."

Bill Kurtis,
Award-winning broadcast journalist

The treasures of the past are fondly revered as new buildings are awaited. The historic Water Tower, built in 1869, best symbolizes what the city is about. It was part of the drive to modernize the booming frontier town and it survived the Great Fire, giving the people hope to rebuild. Today it stands at the head of the Magnificent Mile on Michigan Avenue.

Marking the south end of the Magnificent Mile is the Wrigley Building. Named for the chewing gum magnate, it was built in stages and finished in 1924. The limestone and terra cotta facade forms a gleaming backdrop to events on the Chicago River and the Riverwalk, where people can stroll through a ribbon of parkland all the way to the lakefront.

Wrigley Building

Like most homeowners, Chicago keeps its front yard tidy and makes it a showcase for the city.

The necessities of war have created and recreated Navy Pier. However , the city was not content to allow the mile-long building to languish into dust.

Years of reconstruction have created a family-friendly amusement and entertainment center at Navy Pier. A short ride from the heart of the city, it offers restaurants, dinner lake cruises, rides and concerts.

The revitalized Navy Pier becomes a winter playground

Chicago offers cuisine from every continent to suit every taste.

It's not often we get to sail right into the heart of a city. I had decided to make a sailing tour of the Great Lakes and wanted to be in Chicago for the start of the Mackinac Race. Over the years, I have driven or flown to Chicago, but nothing matches the sensation of sailing right up to the foot of the flashing beacons of the Sears Tower. As I came down from the north, I could see the top of the Sears Tower even before we crossed the state line.

SEVEN-HUNDRED FIFTEEN EAST GRAND AVENUE

After we berthed in Monroe Street Harbor, we headed over to Navy Pier where many of the racing captains and crews were being feted at Riva Restaurant (312-644-7482). We found the atmosphere that of an upscale coastal seafood restaurant. In brass and mahogany decor, we met fresh water and ocean sailors from all points of the compass enjoying a huge selection of lobster and steak dishes Some of the parties were also in private dining rooms.

We could watch our meals being prepared in their large exhibition kitchen, underneath a huge mural showing the history of Navy Pier. Over dinner, we never lost sight of the lake, being enjoyed by pleasure craft of all sizes. In the twilight, the view of the lakefront, Chicago's front yard was awesome. We were doubly lucky to be here on a Wednesday evening because Navy Pier puts on a spectacular fireworks show.

The food lived up to its reputation. I had the Linguini Scampi Diavalo, a zesty dish that lives up to its devilish name - scampi sauteed with garlic, olive oil and crushed red peppers, served with marinara and a touch of cream. My first mate loved the filet mignon of tuna, a marinated and grilled tuna filet, offered on a bed of horseradish mashed potatoes with a roasted shallot sauce and pickled ginger. One famous patron, who just happens to have been president of the United States, once said, "If I knew lunch would be this good, I would have skipped breakfast."

After dinner we swapped sea tales under ceiling fans at the full bar as the moon rose over the lake. Some of these men and women sailors had braved the challenges of rivers, seas and lakes all over the world. In our part of the Riva Restaurant there must have been hundreds of years of experience. We knew Lake Michigan would test their knowledge in the coming days.

Larry and Sandra King,
dairy farmers, Green Bay, Wisconsin

Older neighborhoods, once the bastions of immigrants, dot the city. For its inhabitants, Chicago is a city of neighborhoods. Each neighborhood has its own ethnic parades and festivals. St. Patrick's Day finds the river dyed green and the mayor leading the parade through the center of the city. The snap of fire crackers greets Chinese New Year in Chinatown near Wentworth and Cermak. Cinco de Mayo, Polish Constitution Day, Oktoberfest, Bud Billiken Day, Festa Italiana the list is endless.

A busy Mayor leads one of many ethnic parades.

Sometimes I find myself flying home after some meeting or convention, realizing I haven't seen anything of the city I was in except the four windowless walls of the meeting room or convention hall. Not from Chicago. I was lucky enough to attend a reception at the Crystal Garden on Navy Pier.

PHOTO VIC BIDER

The Crystal Garden takes full advantage of its prime location by bathing its guests with majestic views of the city through its 50-foot atrium windows. From almost a mile out in the lake, we could see a vista that shifted from sail boats plying emerald waters at sunset to the skyline dominated by the Sears Tower sparkling under the stars.

Calling it a garden is a bit of an understatement. We chatted and danced all over this year-round, indoor Eden. palm trees and leap frog fountains, spread over one acre, make the Crystal Garden a real delight for any kind of reception or corporate event.

Outside and only steps away are the giant Ferris wheel and boat rides on the lake and river. the Wave Runner Bar and Grill and the Navy Pier Beer Garden drew lots of people, surrounding us with a carnival atmosphere. Imagine

HOLDING YOUR NEXT MEETING AT THE CENTER OF ALL THIS, A FEW BLOCKS FROM THE LOOP.

THAT REMINDS ME, I'VE GOT TO CALL (312) 595-5446 AND ORGANIZE A SIT-DOWN DINNER FOR 750 FOR MY FRATERNITY'S NATIONAL CONVENTION.

SYDNEY WINTERHAGEN,
COMMODITY BROKER, NEW YORK CITY

NINE FIFTY-ONE NORTH STATE STREET

I ARRIVED IN CHICAGO FOR TWO WEEKS OF MEDICAL LECTURES, BUT WAS DELIGHTED TO DISCOVER THAT I HAD PLENTY OF TIME TO ENJOY THE CITY. FIRST STOP WAS THE SEARS SKYDECK. AS I LOOKED OVER THE STUNNING VIEW OF THIS FABULOUS CITY LAID OUT AT MY FEET, I PLANNED A CULINARY TOUR TO ENJOY THE EVENINGS, AFTER FULL DAYS OF CONFERENCES AND WORKSHOPS.

THE TAVERN ON RUSH SATISFIED ME WONDERFULLY WITH A HUGE STEAK. THE MORE ECLECTIC EATERIES ON RUSH STREET EDUCATED MY TASTE BUDS. HOWEVER, I LOVE LASAGNA AND SOUGHT OUT PAPA MILANO'S AT THE CORNER OF OAK AND STATE. THREE COLLEAGUES AND I WERE GLAD TO FIND A QUIET, COMFORTABLE BOOTH, WHERE WE ENJOYED CHEESE LASAGNA, BAKED CHICKEN MILANO WITH PEAS, MUSHROOMS AND ONIONS. ONE OF THE LADIES FEASTED ON A THIN-CRUST PIZZA WHILE I DECIDED ON A ROSEMARY SALAD AND VEAL FLORENTINE WITH THE FOURTH-GENERATION SICILIAN SAUCE. WE ENJOYED WINE AND CANNOLIS WHILE CHATTING WITH THE PAPA MILANO FAMILY. THEY SUGGESTED A SHORT STROLL TO THE LAKE. WE ENJOYED THE WARM EVENING'S VIEW OF THE CITY FROM OAK STREET BEACH.

MY ONLY REGRET WAS NOT BEING ABLE TO SAMPLE MORE OF THE EXTENSIVE MENU. THAT WAS SHORT-LIVED, HOWEVER. TWO DAYS LATER, WE FOUND OURSELVES BEHIND SCHEDULE SO I SUGGESTED A WORKING LUNCH. WE CALLED 312-787-3710 AND HAD PAPA MILANO DELIVER A WONDERFUL MIDDAY MEAL OF LINGUINI WITH CALAMARI SAUCE, EGGPLANT PARMESAN, PASTA FAGIOL, BAKED CLAMS AND THEIR FAMOUS MEAT LASAGNA. I WILL FIND AN EXCUSE TO VISIT CHICAGO AGAIN, BUT WHO NEEDS ONE?

DR. WOLFGANG KRAMER
DISSELDORF, GERMANY

Visitors also find the Chicago spirit is contagious and far-reaching. Businesses around the world are eager to share in it. Name a business or field and it probably has its convention in Chicago. Travel, sports, consumer electronics, medicine, film, autos, boats, dogs, cats, antiques are all reasons why Chicago greets more people than already live here as business visitors each year.

The crown of light at the top of the John Hancock Building can be seen from three states.

The Magnificent Mile. Chicago's premier real estate becomes a glittering ornament for the winter holidays. The display of light stretches from the river to Lake Shore Drive. A business and hotel district, North Michigan Avenue also boasts premier stores from around the world.

I was staying in Chicago for a series of business meetings and wanted a quick break. I decided to save my energy from my heavy schedule and stuck close to my hotel, the Drake on Michigan Avenue.

I am a fanatic about impressionist art and desperately wanted to get down to the Art Institute. Fortunately, I found a very impressive collection right below me.

Galleries Maurice Sternberg (312-642-1700) is right in the Drake Hotel Arcade on the Magnificent Mile. Only a few steps inside, I forgot about my meetings and was being led through the world of 19th and 20th Century American and European Art by the capable Judith Sternberg. The gallery has been a family business for 55 years and all that experience has been passed to Mrs. Sternberg.

She told me how Chicago had become a center of French Impressionist works when the Palmer family assembled a staggering collection of paintings, most of which are now in the Art Institute. In Galleries Sternberg, I could actually contemplate acquiring a masterwork. Mrs. Sternberg shepherded me through the paintings of Edouard Cortes, Henri Martin and Henri Le Sidaner. Some of these works have been invited to European museum exhibitions. She told me about American painters John George Brown, Hayley Lever and Alexander Calder.

ONE FORTY EAST WALTON PLACE AT MICHIGAN AVENUE

Mrs. Sternberg impressed me not only with her knowledge of art, but her way of learning about a client. She was helping me find a painting that would suit my tastes and lifestyle and was willing to take the time to do it.

I left knowing I'd be back. I had seen a work that would be an important addition to my collection.

Jay Turner,
Art Collector, Park Ridge, Illinois

Winter can mean cold, wind and gloom. But to Chicagoans! It means hot chocolate, ice skating, tobogganing and cross-country skiing. Fun in the snow at almost any city park gives you plenty of excuses to get outdoors to try to catch snowflakes on your tongue.

The Emerald City: Chicago in winter from Lincoln Park Lagoon

Six of us rode a horse-drawn carriage through the area known as River North. After dining at Lino's, we wanted to finish the night off in relaxed style and headed to the Redhead Piano Bar just west of State Street at 16 W. Ontario. We had spotted the "Redhead" sign from the Sears Tower Skydeck earlier in the evening. Just inside, we eased past the busy piano bar into the intimate atmosphere. Walls lined with sheet music and photos of movie greats reverberated from the various standard and pop hits being played. The clientele was well-dressed and the music upbeat. We had a ball, singing along in Chicago's premier piano bar,

Sixteen West Ontario Street

'til the wee hours of the morning. A few weeks later we called (312) 640-1000 to find out who was playing. This time we started the evening at 8 o'clock with cocktails and music at the Redhead. What a great musical evening!

Jon Vanderpellan and friends,
La Grange, Illinois.

All summer long, the Petrillo Band Shell in Grant Park echoes, thunders and dances to music of every taste. You can sit under the stars and let the notes flow like a cool lake breeze. Everyone comes down to the Lakefront and celebrates the Fourth of July with fireworks, food and, of course, jazz.

"When I leave this city, when I leave this earth, the one thing I'll know is this: I lived in a city that truly loved me, and I've loved them."

Michael Jordan

The Kennedy Expressway heads in under the city.

"Close your eyes and feel the city."

Lori Poppa
Accountant
Chicago

"Chicago wants you here. They want you to come. They have so many easy ways into the city. There are no walls, just the lights to guide you into its heart."

Franklin Feinberg
Investor
Tel Aviv, Israel

"Everything is so well planned and laid out. It is so convenient. All the planning of the last century has made a difference."

Erika Eddie
Property Manager
Lucerne, Switzerland

Our daughter was always good with numbers, so it came as no surprise when she told us she wanted to major in accounting. Her choice of schooling did surprise us --- University of Illinois at Chicago. However, we were convinced when she told us how highly regarded the school was. It stands in the shadow of the Sears Tower, a vertical city at the center of Chicago.

Since Charlotte has started school we have made several trips to visit her. Right on the edge of Chicago's "Little Italy" is one of its hidden treasures. Taylor Street is home to many restaurants. Tuscany, our favorite, offers a real family atmosphere which is perfect for us to play catch up. We also meet some great locals, like Ivo Cozzini, who love to share stories about the city, including the history of the neighborhood.

Ten Fourteen West Taylor Street

They will serve your food any way—they just want you to like it. I have seen the waiter carefully going over the menu with a new patron - to find just what they would enjoy. Because the three of us have such different tastes, our waiter suggested an "Italian Sampler" of Vitella All' Aretina (sauteed medallion of veal with sun-dreid tomatoes, goat cheese and pesto), Scampi ai Ferri (marinated grilled scampi) and Petti di Pollo al Palio (grilled breast of chicken with fresh tomatoes, Mozzarella, olive oil and basil). All finished off with Lemon Mandarino for Dessert, we now call Tuscany our "second home".

Mrs. Joseph Hamms,
Insurance Agent, Danville, Illinois

"I love photographing the city at night. It is like opening a chest heaped with treasure. Dazzling!"

David Maenza

State Street stores try to out-decorate each other at Christmas

SOUTH ON MICHIGAN AVENUE FROM THE WATER TOWER

TEN THIRTY-ONE NORTH RUSH STREET

We are new to Chicago. When we heard Norway was playing Japan in women's soccer at Soldier Field, my daughter who goes to Northwestern University wanted to make a big day around this event. A friend suggested a place we had not heard of before.

After the game we went to Tavern on Rush. An interesting name! The name is not fancy, just plain and to the point. But Tavern is very modern and classy. And the food delicious!

Marty, one of the owners, showed us to our table where I had a New York Strip Steak (in Chicago, HA!) with the biggest baked potato I had ever seen. My daughter enjoyed the Shrimp Ciprioni (homemade square noodles in a cognac cream sauce with jumbo shrimp) and my wife dove into some Ahi Tuna. Our friends celebrated over filet Mignon and baby back ribs.

After dinner we moved to an outdoor table to relax and people watch. We watched the city come to life over cappuccino. There was so much happening. Scottie Pippin, the basketball player, stopped in and boy, is he big!

We know we will like it here in Chicago. There is so much excitement.

Tor Hagmo, Import/Exporter, Bergen Norway
(now Lake Shore Drive, Chicago)

"Hog Butcher for the World
Toolmaker, Stacker of Wheat,
Player with Railroads and the
Nation's Freight Handler;
Stormy, husky, brawling
City of the Big Shoulders:..."

Carl Sanburg
Poet

The early days of the National Football League: The Chicago Bears played at Wrigley Field.

North Michigan Avenue: Modern Skyscrapers reach past the historic Water Tower like fingers to the sky.

Lakefront Joggers enjoy the sunrise in front of the newly redesigned Adler Planetarium .

"There can be no better place than this. There just can't."

Lori Garza -
Export coordinator

Gateway to the suburbs: Northwestern Train Station

"Chicago is beautiful.
Pictures don't lie."

Kimberly Gow
University student

Since it was such a clear day, I rented a Limosine to take a tour of the city. Our driver from Metropolitan picked the six of us up at our hotel and suggested we start at the Sears Tower Skydeck. From there we could pick a direction in which to go.

Once at the top, my eldest son, Anders, tried his eight power binoculars and saw a large shopping center to the west. When we came down from the clouds, we asked our driver what Anders could have seen. He told us it was the Oakbrook Shopping Center.

We decided to go there and we enjoyed some great shopping. (We sure did! We packed the trunk!) We decided to have a late lunch and our driver suggested Tuscany Restaraunt in Oakbrook. Tuscany appeared to be a favorite place for the ladies to end their shopping

day. Shoppers come from all the surrounding suburbs like Hinsdale, Wheaton, Winfield and Elmhurst, and nearby states.

We enjoyed Stinco di Vitella Ossobuco (shank of veal with vegetables) And Spaghettini all' Amatriciana (homemade pancetta, sauteed onion, tomato sauce and Parmigiano cheese). My daughters had the grilled Veal chops and Pollo al Vesuvio (1/2 chicken sauteed with garlic, rosemary and white wine). We spoke to Salvatore from Calabria, who had recently visited our homeland. "What a great restaurant!"

Franz Ochermann Family,
Banker, Saas Fee Switzerland

Fourteen Twenty-Five West Twenty-Second Street

"Chicago has all the advantages of a big city and all the charm of a small town. That is the best of both worlds, and this is the best of all cities."

Joan Esposito
TV Newsperson

Marina City

Burnham Harbor at Sunset

"Chicago is so many things. It is a harbor, a Park, big buildings .... and hot-dogs!"

Georg Garkus
Cab Driver
Russia

We called the Metropolitan Limo Co., rented a 12-passenger vehicle and headed for the Morton Arboretum on Route 53 and I-88 in Lisle, IL. Our family enjoyed not only the walk through countless varieties of trees, but the extensive and beautiful gardens. Just for fun, we stopped to shop at various gift shops in Lisle and Naperville. Our hotel concierge had suggested we lunch at Chinn's 34th Street Fishery, "the freshest seafood available!" located at 3011 W. Ogden Ave., in Lisle; 630-637-1777. The proud owner, Stanley Chinn, makes daily trips to the airport to receive and inspect the day's catch.

We were greeted at the door and seated by Stanley's wife, Kim. It was fun checking the shipping orders posted on the entrance bulletin board, certifying the date and delivery from places like Hawaii, Louisiana, Maine and Alaska.

CHINN'S 34TH STREET FISHERY

After Mai Tai's and a basket of rolls dipped in olive oil and fresh garlic, I ordered Australian Rock Lobster Tail. Gunter was served New Zealand Orange Roughy. Our friends and children delighted in having Hawaiian Ahi tuna, Alaskan crab and jumbo shrimp, stuffed with crabmeat and topped with hollandaise sauce. Our server recommended we save room for the special in-house desserts. Key lime or chocolate chip cookie pie, Door County dried cherry bread pudding topped with bourbon sauce and some selections with coconut milk frosting, flown from Hawaii, were just a few.

Kim and Stanley suggested we stroll down Naperville's famous river walk to top off our Chicagoland visit. It was a great day!

Karl Louchter and fellow foresters
Baden Baden, Germany

It was one of those crazy weeknights when the best laid plans of mice and datebooks oft go astray. I had planned to meet friends in Chicago's Old Town neighborhood. Just as I was to leave, they called. Two friends of theirs were in from the Philippines. Where could we go for dinner? I told them I would think of something. As I changed into something more relaxed, I had the answer. It was right there in the heart of the neighborhood.

After we watched the sunset from the Sears Skydeck, we then headed to the Fireplace Inn at 1448 N. Wells in Old Town. For over 30 years this restaurant has devoted itself to serving the best barbecue ribs in the city. And there's seafood. In fact, that made choosing a little difficult for my friends. The combos like ribs and shrimp or ribs and crab satisfied the undecided ones. I went straight for the rib combo. Barbecue heaven was here on earth with chicken and ribs.

In the Fireplace Inn's ski-lodge atmosphere, with stained glass and outdoor garden, I forgot the earlier craziness and relaxed. Later, we moved to Hobos, a little cellar right next door. We enjoyed great conversation over several racks of pool and after-dinner drinks. There was also a huge collection of books and five televisions with nothing but sports.

Fourteen forty-eight North Wells Street

We closed the evening with walk through the lamp light of Old Town. Horse drawn carriages clopped through the turn of the century streets, lined with art galleries and theaters. A stop at the Up/Down Tobacco Shop to pick up my favorite Old Maid tobacco gave my friends a chance to select some fine cigars.

In a social emergency, I toss the datebook out the window and call the Fireplace Inn at (312) 664-5264 and they deliver my salvation.

Norman Ross
TV personality

A CIRCLE OF ELEVATED TRAIN LINES FORMS THE FAMOUS LOOP THAT CONNECTS WITH A MODERN TRANSPORTATION SYSTEM REACHING ALL PARTS OF THE CITY AND SUBURBS INCLUDING TWO MAJOR AIRPORTS.

Professional teams in every major sport excite fans in modern venues throughout the city. The Chicago Bears do battle on the grid-iron at Soldier Field. The Chicago Bulls basketball team shares the United Center with hockey's Chicago Blackhawks.

Chicago loves the national pastime so much that one baseball team is not enough.

The Chicago Cubs and White Sox play day and night games throughout the summer.

Both ballparks are located minutes away by elevated train or bus from the Loop.

Dedicated fans are not just spectators, they are part of the show at Wrigley Field and Comiskey Park.

"Alright now, let me hear ya"!

Thanks, Harry

Sammy Sosa hits Number 56 on his way to a record 66 home runs. "Chicago, I love you."

THIRTY-SEVEN HUNDRED NORTH CLARK STREET

We visited Chicago to see our baseball team battle the Chicago Cubs for a weekend series. We cabbed over to Wrigleyville early, so we would have time to see this interesting neighborhood before the game. A stone's throw (or should I say, a home run) from the ball park is Tuscany on Clark, (773)-404-7700 at the corner of Clark and Waveland. The hostess seating us noticed our Cardinal jackets and gave us a run-down of how our players might do against the Cubs. Not surprising in a neighborhood named after a ball park.

Surrounded by wine bottles and Italian ceramics, our table was fun and festive with dishes like Spaghettini ala Marcellino (pasta with garlic, olive oil, shrimp, scallops, fresh spinach and roasted peppers) and Pettichi pollo alla Valdostana (chicken breast stuffed with prosciutto and fontina cheese in a special wine sauce).

As we dined on the outdoor patio, we saw fans buying pennants, baseball caps and numbered jerseys of their favorite players. I reminisced about seeing the Cubs play the Tigers in the World Series as a boy. We then strolled across the street to the classic Wrigley Field and watched an exciting game under the lights, cooled by a wonderful lake breeze.

Mr. and Mrs. Harry Sullivan,
Consultant- retired, St. Louis, Missouri

Four major marinas , serving both power and sailing craft, line Chicago's Lakefront

A lucky couple may even have Lake Michigan all to themselves.

THE LAKE WILL REMAIN.

THROUGH A MIRACLE OF ENGINEERING AND THE DEVOTION OF THE CITY, THE LAKE STAYS PRISTINE, TOUCHED ONLY BY THE BOATS WHO SAIL IT AND SWIMMERS WHO COOL OFF IN IT.

FOURTY-SEVEN THIRTY-TWO NORTH LINCOLN AVENUE

I never let more than a few months go by without a pilgrimage to the "old neighborhood" at Lincoln Square. I recently took the family back to the intersection of Lincoln, Lawrence and Western Avenues, which still echoes of the old world. A short ride north from the Sears Tower are sidewalk cafés, with people enjoying coffee and pastries. The steady stream of shoppers leaving Meyer's Delicatessen with German meats, breads and other delicacies reminds me of Munich.

It does not get any more German than the Chicago Brauhaus, our goal for a long, leisurely lunch. Harry and Guenter Kempf have made the Brauhaus a favorite for locals and visitors; a place for relaxation and unmatched meals. Harry greeted us as always, but soon disappeared into the kitchen to create traditional dishes including wiener schnitzel, roulade,

ROAST DUCKLING, RED CABBAGE AND SAUERKRAUT. WE STARTED OFF WITH LARGE STEINS FILLED WITH ONE OF THE MANY IMPORTED BEERS IN THIS BAVARIAN ATMOSPHERE. BEFORE LONG THE TABLE WAS CROWDED WITH ORDERS OF PORK SCHNITZEL, KASSLER RIPPCHEN, AND BOILED PORK SHANK WHILE THE MUSIC PLAYED ON. BUT WE STILL HAD ROOM FOR APPLE STRUDEL WITH WHIPPED CREAM AND PLUM KUCHEN. I EVEN LEARNED A NEW WORD: AUSGEZEICHNET! EXCELLENT!

WE LOVE TO COME DOWN ON SUMMER NIGHTS FOR ONE OF THE FESTIVALS ON LINCOLN PLAZA AND ENJOY THE BRATWURST FROM THE BRAUHAUS JUST ACROSS THE STREET. NATURALLY, WE WOULDN'T MISS OKTOBERFEST. A CALL TO (773) 784-4444 GETS US RESERVATIONS FOR THE CHRISTMAS CELEBRATIONS WITH SINGING GROUPS IN COLORFUL COSTUMES AND EUROPEAN DECORATIONS FROM THE LOCAL SCHOOLS. EVERY NIGHT THERE IS DANCING AS GUENTER AND HARRY DELIGHT THEIR PATRONS WITH GERMAN FAVORITES.

IT WON'T BE LONG 'TIL WE'RE BACK.

THE HALE FAMILY,
PARK RIDGE, ILLINOIS

O'Hare International Airport, home of United Airlines 1-800-241-6522 and Hilton Chicago O'Hare 1-800-HILTONS

Throughout the twentieth century, Chicago has never relinquished its crown as a transportation hub. As air travel replaced trains as the chief mode of transportation, the city expanded westward, taking over an old military airfield after World War II in a far-sighted move. The airport's designator, ORD, comes from its original name: Orchard Place, but the field was soon renamed to honor Lieutenant Commander Edward "Butch" O'Hare. O'Hare was a naval pilot from Chicago who received the Congressional Medal of Honor for bravery after being killed in the Pacific during the war.

Chicago's spirit to constantly remake itself is reflected in the development of this ultra-modern

facility. It lengthened its runways as the jet age dawned. In the 70's, the O'Hare Hilton Hotel was built as a haven for harried travelers just steps from the terminals through underground tunnels. In the 80's and 90's , O'Hare completely renovated its terminals to accommodate the soaring passenger rates.

Today O'Hare Field is still the busiest airport in the world with over 70 million passengers yearly traveling to and from all continents, on major carriers such as British Airways, American, Cathay Pacific, Iberia and Royal Jordanian Air. It also is a cargo gateway for tons of goods for every corner of the globe.

"It reminds me of the crown jewels in the tower of London. It sparkles and dazzles. Diamonds, rubies and emeralds laid out at your feet."

Franklin King
Boxing Promoter
London

As soon as we walked in the door I knew Manny's had character. It was populated by businessmen from the area just south of downtown. I studied the 45-foot menu board as I slid my tray along the cafeteria style counter. I had no idea what to pick, but I knew that, whatever I would ask for, I would get plenty of it.

Manny's deserves its status as an eating landmark. For over 50 years, 35 at this location at 1141 S. Jefferson Street, Chicagoans have been coming here to eat, not dine on sprigs and twigs, but EAT. Plates piled high with pastrami, roast beef, the biggest and best corned beef in Chicago served with a potato pancake and a must - Lake Superior Whitefish chased by Cheesecake and pies. You come here to get un-hungry. Ken Raskin, the third generation owner, will see that you do.

We were surrounded by nostalgia in this retro-50's diner that is the noon home of the neighborhood locals. Newspaper clippings line the walls, showing a family business growing by keeping its family traditions. They used to have a van that circled the neighborhood making deliveries. It never came back empty—it picked up customers for lunch. Manny's still delivers. You can call (312) 939-2855 and they'll bring in Lunch for a dozen or a hundred.

You'll find all the deli standards on the huge 45-foot menu board—pickled beets, marinated cucumbers, Rueben sandwiches and gefilte fish. I decided not to bother reading it at all. I asked my stomach what it wanted. It said a Rueben, chocolate phosphate and cheesecake. I got it. When we were done, it said "thanks, Manny's".

Matt Greenstein, Publisher,
Downtown Chicago

"From the top of the Sears Tower, one might believe the streets are paved with gold."

Paul Collins
Designer

"Visitors arrive uncertain. They leave enamored."

Wally Philips
Radio Personality

The Field Museum of Natural History is a center of on-going research into dinosaurs and prehistoric man.

Over the years, we have carefully selected several restaurants which have the style and menu that we like to include in our evenings, by ourselves or with friends, often after the theater or opera. We had just enjoyed a fabulous performance at the Lyric Opera House and planned to finish the evening at one of our favorites.

Tsunami means "great wave" in Japanese, but in Chicago it means authentic Japanese cuisine at the Tsunami restaurant. Tsunami blends the energy of modern Japan with ancient traditions that stretch over a thousand years.

The upstairs Sake Lounge was electric with post modern decor that stimulates conversation. Old friends related their excitement over the latest play or symphony they had enjoyed. One of our group met a lady he had known on and off over the years. We weren't surprised when they found an intimate table inside amongst antique art while we moved outside to the sidewalk café.

Traditions developed over centuries to bring out the flavors of Sushi and Sushimi are alive and respected here. Over our appetizers of shrimp and vegetable tempura, we watched the crowds from nearby Rush Street ebb and flow like a great sea. Sushi and sake with sesame essence beef tenderloin with lobster mashed potato, sugar snap peas and teriyaki sauce were carefully prepared by expert chefs along with selections of Nigiri and Maki Mono. We also availed ourselves of Tsunami's extensive wine list - a rarity in Japanese restaruants.

Tsunami's phone number, (312)642-9911, is permanently in our list of places we enjoy often. They offer a pure point of view of Japanese food, tempered with just the right mix of western tastes - the best of both worlds.

Mr. and Mrs. David Wrigley,
Restoration Architect, Lake Forest, Illinois

Eleven Sixty North Dearborn Street

"I've been traveling the world since the early Sixties when the only thing people thought about Chicago was "Al Capone Land". Now, it's not unusual to hear first-time visitors refer to Chicago as "that wonderful city by the lake". And why shouldn't they? Ours truly is a wonderful and proud city - it is very clean with a fabulous lakefront, numerous beautifully sculpted parks and distinctive architecture.

"We have a thriving business center, world-class restaurants and, most of all, a diverse cultural community with first-rate museums, the Chicago Symphony Orchestra, the Lyric Opera, an ever-growing theater community and world-class dance companies... and I haven't even gotten to our music scene, including our much envied jazz and blues clubs.

"We are not without our problems - what major cities these days are? But the difference is that we have the courage to confront our problems and strive to work them out. We are the finest example today of great ideas and great people. We call it... Chicagoland!"

Ramsey E. Lewis Jr.

Chicago will remain dedicated to people. Those who live here and those who visit will always be able to play or work here and to find heart pounding excitement or quiet solitude.

Romantic walk: the "Golden Collar" near Lake Shore Drive.

The Chicago of stone and steel will not remain fixed forever. The seeds of the city's future are sown everyday. The skyline seems to change monthly as construction cranes pirouette to a constant, driving theme. Daring designs arc to the clouds and are filled with people with new ideas and visions.

"I love seeing Chicago change to more beautiful architecture each visit."

Daniel Beederman
Attorney

Four of us took the train in from Birmingham, Michigan. It always gives me a thrill to arrive at Union Station with its dramatic neo classical interior. Not many people know that Chicago is still a major rail hub.

During the roughly six hour trip in first class accomodations, we watched the Midwest roll by. We arrived in Chicago rested and eager to start our list of places to visit in town. Our friend, Mike picked us up and called (312) 266-0616 and 10 minutes later we were seated at Lino's Restaurant.

Our table was surrounded by the beautiful art and photographs of Italy, especially Florence. The wine was a perfect complement to dishes like Vitella Valdostana, (stuffed Veal Chop), Tagliata di Manzo ai Ferri (16oz. New York Steak slice, with fresh Garlic and Rosemary) and Pesce al Sale (whole fish of the day baked in a crust of salt).

TWO TWENTY-TWO WEST ONTARIO STREET

Everyone at Lino's made sure we enjoyed our meal. It was exciting to sample recipes brought here from all over Italy.

After dinner, we walked a few blocks and topped the evening off singing at the Red Head Piano bar until they closed. That's how we started our weekend!

Bill Wedell, Gymnastic Coach,
Rochester Hills, Michigan

We've just returned from an extended stay in Mexico. After celebrating New Years in Mexico City, we enjoyed Carnival in Veracruz. Then we had two short weeks photographing the pelicans and enjoying the winter sun in Mazatlán. In Puerto Vallarta we decided that we had a real love for Mexico.

On a double decker bus tour of Chicago, we passed the new statue of Juárez near the Wrigley Building. It reminded us that we hadn't had a real Mexican dinner in weeks. As the bus tour headed up Michigan Avenue, we decided to meet some friends at Salpicón in Old Town, about a mile from the Sears Tower.

Moments after arriving, we felt as if we were dining in someone's home in Mexico City. Salpicón is breath takingly decorated with paintings and ceramics. Our friends called (312) 988-7811 to see if we had arrived. As I answered the phone, they were pulling up in a Noble horse drawn carriage—complete with cellular phone.

Dinner was like reliving our stay in Mexico. Pollo en Mole Poblano, half of an Amish chicken was served in a classic Pueblan mole sauce with mexican rice for my wife and me. Our friends enjoyed their favorite: Seviche de Camarón y Pulpo con Aguacate, a spicy shrimp and octopus seviche marinated in orange and lime juices with habanero chiles.

We know we have found a portal back to Old Mexico that we can visit anytime we are in Chicago, so many dishes to try!

Richard Newberry, retired shoe store owner,
Pittsburgh, Pennsylvania.

The heart of the city is not just sterile steel and glass. It is a constant celebration of the soul of the city - people. Parades, festivals and music are all part of daily life in the financial and business districts of the "Loop". Even after business hours and on weekends people stay downtown for theaters, restaurants and even a ride in a horse-drawn carriage.

Fiesta on State Street

4th of July Fireworks follow the conductor&s baton to the ~1812 Overture~

The people are the future. They will change; new visitors and city dwellers will arrive. They will leave their mark in some way that will become inevitably Chicagoan. In exchange the "I WILL" spirit will grow into everything they do or dream.

Echoes of yesterday

Michigan Avenue Bridge over the Chicago River

"It's like a pilgrimage. We wait for that first great day in the spring and take our boats to the beautiful lake. When the last bridge goes up, we're set free."

Dr. Harold Arai
Dentist
Park Ridge

"The Firecrackers! The food! I am so happy we were here for Chinese New year in Chinatown. Only Shanghai would be better."

James DeGuzman
Farmer
The Philippines

"It is so hard to imagine what has happened here. Nothing but marshes and grass, then came settlers with tents and shacks. And then the Fire. I wish the people standing in the ashes could see this.... who knows? Somehow maybe they did. And that is why the city's here."

Benjamin Miles
Cowboy
Minot, North Dakota

Merchandise Mart

Museum of Science and Industry

"I have to come back four more times. First time I saw just the museums. There is so much in just one of them."

Charles Farina
Boat Captain
Sardinia

Marriott

FOURTEEN EIGHTEEN WEST FULLERTON PARKWAY

I'VE GOT TO SAY THIS IS ONE FAST MOVING CITY. YOU NEVER KNOW WHO YOU'LL MEET, RUB SHOULDERS WITH OR GET AN AUTOGRAPH FROM. ALL OVER THE LINCOLN PARK AREA, THEY'RE SHOOTING MOVIES AND TV SERIES. LAST TIME WE WERE IN TOWN, WE SAW MARK GRACE AND GOLDIE HAWN. AT STEFANI'S, A GREAT NEAR NORTH RESTAURANT, WE CAUGHT A GLIMPSE OF A MAN WITH A TRUE "FOLLOWING".

AFTER ENJOYING A DAY AT THE LINCOLN PARK ZOO, OUR CAB BROUGHT US OVER TO STEFANI'S ON FULLERTON. ARRIVING AT THE SAME TIME, A MAN WITH A CLERICAL COLLAR AND A BROAD SMILE WAVED TO SEVERAL PEOPLE. INSIDE THEY TOLD US HE WAS FRANCIS CARDINAL GEORGE, ARCHBISHOP OF CHICAGO. WE FIGURED IF STEFANI'S WAS GOOD ENOUGH FOR THE ARCHBISHOP, IT'S GOOD ENOUGH FOR US PROTESTANTS FROM BOSTON.

WE REALLY ENJOYED THE APPETIZER OF POLPI PICCANTINI ALLA GRIGLIA (GRILLED, MARINATED BABY OCTOPUS). WHILE WE DINED IN THEIR OUTDOOR GARDEN, SURROUNDED BY BEAUTIFUL FLOWERS AND FESTIVE ITALIAN MUSIC, WE ENJOYED OUR ENTREE OF FETTUCCINE AL SAPORE DI VERDURE, (GRILLED CHICKEN BREAST OVER FETTUCCINE WITH GRILLED VEGETABLE PESTO) AND A GLASS OR TWO OF LUNGORATTI ROBESCO, A FINE ITALIAN WINE.

THE OWNER, PHIL STEFANI, STOPPED BY PERSONALLY TO ASK HOW WE LIKED OUR FOOD AND SUGGESTED WE MIGHT CATCH A PLAY ON HALSTED STREET AFTER DINNER. I NEEDED A ROOM FOR AN UPCOMING

PHOTO VIC BIDER

corporate meeting, and took the opportunity to ask him about it. A quick look around and our dinners convinced me I needed to look no further. Stefani's has several rooms for private dining occasions and meetings. I made a note to call him at (773) 348-0111.

After dinner we saw a great play at the Steppenwolf Theater, which we laughed at for two hours straight! A magnificent evening!

Kevin Milford, Attorney,
Boston, Massachusetts

Chicago's heart pulses to the beat of music. Blues, Gospel, Jazz, Classical and Opera. One of the birthplaces of the fabled art, Chicago boasts Blues venues with star performers side by side with up-and-coming musicians.

The Lyric Opera and Chicago Symphony Orchestra are homes to a wide range of talented artists. Music festivals for every taste span the entire year.

"Chicago writes its own music. It moves to its own beat and gets into your soul."

Bob Hale
Chicago Broadcaster

The city's mind has its needs, too. In the aftermath of the Great Chicago Fire of 1871, an Englishman, Thomas Hughes, organized the donation of 8,000 books to the city. The donations included gifts from Queen Victoria, Benjamin Disraeli, Alfred Lord Tennyson and Robert Browning. They seeded a collection that became the millions of volumes now in the Chicago Public Library's 78 locations. Acclaimed for its daring neo-classical architecture, the anchor Harold Washington Library Center at 400 S. State Street, is one of the foremost educational and cultural resources in Chicago.

"Monument with Standing Beast"
by Jean Dubuffet
at State of Illinois Building

"Why do they make the river green and who was this Saint Patrick?"

Dr. J. Harrani
Maldives

"The bridges are amazing! They all swing up like swans raising their necks to salute the boats."

Martha Thylin
Pharmacist
Stockholm

Lake Michigan: Pristine waters for swimming and boating

And there will always be the parks and the design of a city in a garden. They will improve and change to fit new lifestyles and peoples.

Chicago, 1980

"There is one thing about Chicago that is constant. Change. The City seems always eager to grow and outdo itself. Restless, it greets the dawn everyday with its eyes looking upward. Bigger, better, faster. It seems sometimes the energy spills over into the electrical storms that light up the sky here. In the song the city is called "toddling". Children toddle. Chicago is a large zesty youth. Its toddling days are over."

Marylin Mooney
United Kingdom

"In one word.... BOOM! Like a rocket. That's what I think of Chicago."

John Leeman
Fisherman
Nova Scotia

Oak Street Beach

"I was surprised you could swim here. Not a hundred meters from a huge city and I stand in pure, clean water."

Vincent Farchie
Soccer Player
Bologna, Italy

Shedd Aquarium

"At the Shedd Aquarium, they have a forest ... inside a building! It is brilliant, just how it blends right into the view of the lake."

Michael Bartley
Javelin Thrower
Cliffs of Mohr, Ireland

View into the "Loop" from the west

I lost my suitcase and had business at the Merchandise Mart. Fortunately, the A&G Clothing Store in the Mart had a great selection of European designs. I called Howard Goldberg at (312) 245-0377 and thanked him for all his help.

Antonio Lazzari
Rome

PHOTO VIC BIDER

It was a quiet winter day when I passed the Picasso sculpture in the Daley Civic Center plaza for probably the thousandth time. Since its arrival in 1967, the enigmatic piece has charmed Chicagoans and added to the wonderful collection of public artworks that grace the Loop. It is such a familiar object now, but it still held a certain mystery. Sometimes to really understand a work, it helps to see the environment which shaped the artist.

Iberia airlines and the Spanish Tourist Office in Chicago guided me to the Costa del Sol, the Sun Coast. I found it was perfectly named. Weather geography and history have all conspired to create a paradise of Moorish mystique, mixed with Spanish spice, along the Marbella - Málaga coast. Basing myself at the Gran Melia Don Pepe Hotel in Marbella, I set out to discover what could have inspired the master.

Flowers draping iron-railed balconies contrast white-washed buildings in Marbella's Old City of narrow winding streets. I discovered a wonderful spanish tradition, Tapas, in the Restaurante Santiago, located in the Paseo Martímo in Marbella. Owner Santiago Domingez was a culinary tour guide,

taking me through a seven course Andalusian feast of Dorada a La Espalda, a sea bass specialty.

The Moors and Romans left their indelible marks on this crossroads between east and west. A moorish castle was the heart of Marbella. Roman ruins with mosaics and other artifacts dot the surrounding land near Ronda.

But it was the energy of the people that most impressed me. They celebrate life and gifts of nature with festivals and fiestas in Mijas and other towns around Marbella. I could see and hear this energy daily in the passion and thunder of the flamenco dance at Café de Chinitas in Madrid. I wondered if Picasso might have been as moved as I was.

While in Madrid, I wanted to visit the famed Museo del Prado. Just steps from my rooms at the Villa Real Hotel I found the works of Goya, Vasquez and, of course, Picasso. More history I found at the Botin, a 250 year-old reastaraunt where the food is cooked in the same way as when the mosaic walls and beamed ceilings were new.

Back in Chicago I quickly began to miss Spain. I found a piece of it not far away, just north at 739 N. La Salle Street, I found an oasis of Spanish food and culture at Iberico, a restaurant

"It looks like my wife."

Jack Von Buring
Construction company owner
Worms, Germany

"Beautiful? I do not know. It is like a fountain of steel."

Silvia Mendoza
Candlemaker
Mexico City

"Picasso, Miro, Chagall.... Chicago is a museum of art! The whole city!"

Penelope Mevrelos
Nurse
Athens, Greece

famous for its Tapas.

Tapas is more than a type of cuisine; it is a warm atmosphere of friends and conversation that surrounds these small portions, served with wine, beer or, especially, Sangria. I was taken by the variety of delicious foods, especially Gampas al Ajillo (grilled shrimp with garlic sauce), that seemed to be full of the energy of Spain, served in such a way so that friends can enjoy each other's company as well as the meal.

Iberico's owner, Jose Lagoa, faithfully imports many of the ingredients, complete with their tradition. Grilled Calamari, Baked goat cheese in tomato sauce, octopus and shrimp, seasoned with imported spices, oils and olives direct from Spain instantly transport you there. There's even live Spanish TV. Patrons enjoy Flamenco dancers and soccer direct from the old world. I was only a little surprised to see Placido Domingo enjoying an evening with friends at Iberico.

I went back to the Picasso and saw it had changed. It was now part sun, part spice and all the energy I had found in the master's homeland.

Photographer, David Maenza

"They don't call it the Windy City for nothing. But if you don't like the weather in Chicago, just wait a minute. It'll change."

Unknown

Photo of the Wrigley Building from Roosevelt Road and South Michigan avenue

The Heart of the City: Buckingham Fountain in Grant Park

For dinner, the concierge at our hotel suggested we cab to the best French restaurant in town called La Sardine. Found in the West loop area at 111 N. Carpenter, it's across the street from Oprah Winfrey's Harpo Studio. Thoroughly pleased with the enticing setting, excellent service and great chef, we returned the next day to the hustle and bustle of our great new find. Our CEO ordered Le Steak Grillé Maitre d'Hotel, grilled steak with house butter and homemade fries. Mr. Franks, who is in charge of purchasing, enjoyed La Bouillabaisse "Jean-Claude". I chose the Red Snapper with English Peas, enhanced by a glass of Sancere. The amenities were superb, the open grill fun to observe. Absolutely delightful! 312-421-2800

Richard Hunt, Shipping Manager,
Wellington, New Zealand

After an exhausting day of antique hunting in the Bucktown neighborhood, We discovered one of the most popular french bistros in Chicago, Le Bouchon at 1958 North Damen. Tucked into a tiny storefront, it looked perfect. We quickly phoned 773-862-6600 to find out if reservations were needed and were immediately accommodated. What a treat...small, friendly and totally Parisian.

Mr. Peter Altgeld
Antique Buyer,
Portland, Oregon

Wrigley Building and bridges, over the Chicago River, completed in 1924

Afternoon view from the Shedd Aquarium

"It's always great to see the various colored cloudy panoramas, so many shapes, so much beauty!."

Don Altieri, Lithographer
Fran Altieri, Bank Officer
Northbrook, IL

Modern Burnham Harbor

A historic panorama photo of Chicago, 01:01:2000.

2000

"I flew over the newly renovated Belmont Harbor"

Brad Cavanaugh-Air One

"Looking at the lake on an early summer morning, I feel as if I'am in paradise."

Agnes Santomarco
Structural Steel, sales lady
New York City